My Journey
to
Salvation

My Journey
to
Salvation

Joe Hancock

To order additional copies of this book, contact:
Xlibris Corporation
1-888-795-4274
www.Xlibris.com
Orders@Xlibris.com
111764

CONTENTS

I dedicate this book to my loving wife of 59 years 3 months and 10 days until Jesus took her home to life eternal. Also a special thanks to my granddaughter Kristina Gold And my daughters Shirley Mertz and Theresa Morlock who encouraged me to expand the writing about my path of life leading to my salvation and helped with the editing of it.

Joe Hancock
1950 pre marriage photo

Leona Mowery
1950 pre marriage photo

INTRODUCTION

My Churchless Youth

Born in 1933 I grew up having no church or Sunday school training. Things were very harsh during the depression and WW2. During that time I learned much of the good and evil the world had to offer. As a teenager I worked Mondays to Fridays from 7 PM until 11 PM setting pins at the local bowling alley and weekends at a filling station pumping gas and washing cars. My desire for a better life grew strong during this time. In high school during my senior year, being in a CO-OP program, I was placed with a large manufacturer in the Tool Design department. In this position I learned fast and did very well. It was during this time I met and fell in love, later married, and shared 59 years 3 months and 10 days with my soul mate until Jesus called her home to be with him. Yes, deep sorrow at first but I know joy will return when my Sweet Pea and I meet in the morning just inside the Eastern Gate over there.

Having proposed to and accepted by Leona my wife to be we decided to elope. Leona left home which caused her parents to take action. Being on the lam so to speak, we hid out on my uncle's farm for 3 days. My Uncle Ted Hancock and Aunt Francis then drove us to Indiana where we were married by a Justice of the peace. Returning home Ted stopped at a bar where Ted and I had a drink to celebrate. Being married, [everyone we knew told us it would not last] we then spent several months living with my parents before buying a house trailer as our first home. Shortly after our first child was born we purchased a larger trailer. Months later we sold the trailer and rented a home in my hometown Sidney. During this time we attended movies at the local drive-in and went dancing at the local Eagles club. To be sure we had our spats and ups and downs during this time. Most importantly we always talked through such problems.

Early in our marriage my wife met and became friends with a neighborhood Christian lady. Raised a catholic my wife joined the neighbor's church and was saved at a revival meeting. The wife and friends then tried talking to me about Jesus. Unknown to me during that time and until I was saved they held many prayer meetings asking Jesus to save me.

During this time, being sin filled and enjoying it, I would have no part of their lord Jesus, I was busy building a career for our future. We were blessed with children, in 1951 a girl [Shirley], in 1952 a boy [Michael], in 1960 a boy [Patrick], in 1963 a girl [Theresa] and in 1969 a boy [Timothy]. During the years 1950 to 1955 I worked in Sidney then moved to Dayton in our new trailer where I worked several years before selling the trailer In Dayton and renting a home in Sidney and taking a Job in Jackson Center. It was in 1955 having much improved my skills and training I started a job with a jet engine parts manufacturer as a tool designer. It was here I met a Born Again christen gentleman 20 years my senior. Little did I know we would become lifelong friends? His name was Kent Stemen. Kent and other Christian workers talked to me about Jesus.

CHAPTER 1

Bible at Age 23

Because I was showing little interest Kent gave me a pocket size new testament King James Bible and encouraged me to read it. During the next 4 years, slowly at first and then at a faster pace I was reading daily which led me to a great many questions. During this time I joined Kent and his friends during lunchtime, as they would take turns reading the scriptures aloud to the group The group tried to help me understand the many concerns I continued to bring up to them. Such as how one can be sure they are born again or how does the holy spirit work in believers lives or can I be saved then sin and be dammed or how do I know God hears my prayers or must I join a church or if once saved I cannot be lost but can still commit sin or one says this and another seems to contradict it.

During that time the answers I was given fit perfectly with the scriptures we were reading. Slowly my understanding of the Bible was taking shape. It was at this time I started understanding how important context is in scripture study and later discovered finding a keyword or keywords can lead to a better understanding of who God is and his rules for living in this world. Although this is ahead of my story it is here I wish to give examples of keywords.

CHAPTER 2

KEYWORDS

In scripture study when one establishes the context of a scripture verse of interest or one that you do not understand an often overlooked guide to help lies in finding a keyword or keywords within that scripture verse. It is here I will give a few examples of keywords I have found, starting in the Garden of Eden it is written in

> [Genesis 3]
> 2Then the woman said to the serpent, we may eat of the fruit of the trees of the garden
> 3But of the fruit of the tree which is in the midst of the garden, God has said, you shall not eat of it, neither shall you touch it, lest you die.

Yes Eve was beguiled however I note her saying, [neither shall you touch it]. The only record of God giving a warning about the tree was before EVE was created when he warned Adam as written in

> [Genesis 2]
> 7But of the tree of the knowledge of good and evil, you must not eat of it for in the day that you eat thereof you shall surely die.

It is my opinion Adam in telling Eve about the tree sinned by adding these words to Gods command, [neither shall you touch it]. And so mans first freewill act of rebellion by adding to Gods command starts the journey of the human races fall from grace. For the next example see the story of Jehu having Jezebel killed as written in

[2 Kings 9]

³¹Then as Jehu entered in at the gate, she said, Had Zimri peace, who killed his master?

³²Then he lifted up his face to the window, and said who is on my side? Who? And there looked out to him two or three eunuchs.

³³And he said, Throw her down. So they threw her down and some of her blood was sprinkled on the wall, and on the horses and he trod her under foot.

Take note of the words [two or three eunuchs]. Eunuchs are servants but why say two or three? It is my opinion number three is of special note and must be a chief servant. Because the written scriptures say Jesus came as a servant for matters such as this in

[Isaiah 42]

¹Behold my servant, whom I uphold; mine elect, in whom my soul delights; I have put my spirit upon him he shall bring forth judgment to the Gentiles.

Because scholars perceive Jesus appeared at various times in the Old Testament I believe this third eunuch was the Lord Jesus Christ.

Let us now look at the rescue of Moses story written in

[Exodus 2]

¹⁰Because the child grew, and she brought him to Pharaoh's daughter, and he became her son. And she called his name Moses and she said, because I drew him out of the water.

This was a rescue from certain death ordered by Pharaoh as written in

[Exodus 1]

¹⁵Then the king of Egypt spoke to the Hebrew midwives, of which the name of the one was Shiphrah, and the name of the other Puah

[16]Then he said, When you do the office of a midwife to the
Hebrew women, and see them upon the stools; if it be a son, then
you shall kill him but if it be a daughter, then she shall live.

Haven given context let us now look to a keyword of interest written in

[Exodus 2]
[11]And it came to pass in those days, when Moses was grown,
that he went out to his brethren, and looked on their burdens and
he spied an Egyptian smiting a Hebrew, one of his brethren.

Here my interest falls on the keyword "brethren". Having given context for
this passage it is my opinion Moses was told by his mother he was born a
Hebrew and so he knew the Hebrews were his brethren.

Let it here be known that the study of keywords may seem trivial to some,
but, it does however lead to increasing ones knowledge of how God makes
good results occur from the evil events that are taking place. That being
said let us look at a hidden keyword written in

[John 3]
[5]Jesus answered. Truly, Truly I say to you, except a man
is born of water by a woman and of the Spirit from above, he
cannot enter into the kingdom of God.
[6] That which is born of the flesh is flesh; and that which is
born of the Spirit is spirit.
[7] Marvel not that I said to You, You must be born again.

We know every child born comes into this world after the mother's water
breaks. The point of interest I see is Jesus saying, "Born of the spirit".
While Nicodemus asked how one can be born again my point of interest is
what this spirit is. To find the answer I first must know what is this spirit
and where do I find it written. I started here in

[Colossians 2]
[2]That their hearts might be comforted, being knit together
in love, and to all riches of the full assurance of understanding, to
the acknowledgement of the mystery of God, and of the Father,
and of Christ.

³In whom are hidden all the treasures of wisdom and knowledge.

I now know the spirit is hidden but where, the answer is written in

[Romans 8]
¹There is therefore now no condemnation to them which are in Christ Jesus; who walk not after the flesh but after the Spirit.

We now know the spirit is found in Christ Jesus. The last question, what is this spirit? I find it written in

[Isaiah 11]
²And the spirit of the Lord shall rest upon him, the spirit of wisdom and understanding, the spirit of counsel and might, the spirit of knowledge and of the fear of the Lord;

It is here I understand to be born again and walk in the spirit of Christ Jesus the believer also shares the attributes of his spirit to guide and sustain ones path in life while growing in the grace and knowledge of God and his son Jesus Christ.

And now read a deeply hidden keyword written in

[Matthew 7]
²²Many will say to me in that day, Lord, Lord, have we not prophesied in your name? And in your name have cast out devils? And in your name done many wonderful works?
²³Then will I profess to them, I never knew you depart from me, you that work iniquity.

The keyword is iniquity. Many say it is sin but if it is only sin why not say sin. My spirit says, yes sin, but a very special type of sin. I found my answer written in

[1ˢᵗ Samuel 15]
²³Because rebellion is as the sin of witchcraft and stubbornness is as iniquity and idolatry. Because thou hast rejected the word of the Lord, he hath also rejected thee from being king.

Sadly I realize Iniquity and Idolatry are a spiritual Stubbornness toward God. By putting Stubbornness and Idols first in life [That which controls one's life] helps explain the multitude of religions and churches found throughout the world which tells me a multitude of professing believers still walk in the flesh. When judgment day comes it is written Jesus forewarns all in

> [St. Luke 13]
> 24"Strive to enter through the narrow gate, for many, I say to you, will seek to enter and will not be able.

Having given these few references my intent is to try showing how important careful study of context and phrases or a single word can be in helping one search out a fuller understanding and knowledge for this "Age of Grace" given us by God and his son Jesus Christ.

[Now let's return to my story] Not that I understood everything but I began to realize things were not right in my life.

CHAPTER 3

Sin Confessed

At this point in my life I understood how sinful and lost I was. I visited a revival meeting one night in my hometown and went forward at the invitation to receive Jesus Christ as my savior. My going forward to the altar did not help. It was during this period of my life I understood I knew about Jesus but was not saved. To such a dilemma I find this written in

> [Deuteronomy 30]
> [19]I call heaven and earth to record this day against you, that I have set before you life and death, blessing and cursing therefore choose life, that both you and your seed may live

I also find this written in

> [John 3]
> [3]Jesus answered and said to him, truly, truly, I say to you, Except a man be born again, he cannot see the kingdom of God.

It was during this time, the spring of 1960, I found a quite place and had a heart to heart talk with God. It was here I finally realized my life was filled with all kinds of lust and sinful thoughts of many things. Shortly after this while on my way to work in Lima, ridding with a coworker, I suddenly became aware of the spiritual presence of an Angel that spoke to me in a strong but still small voice saying, Joe I want you to become a preacher of my word.

I then turned to Jesus confessing my known and unknown sins and asked Jesus to save me. Please note why this is written In

> [Mark 16]
> ¹⁶He that believes and is born from above shall be saved; but he that believes not shall be damned.

Strangely at that moment there was no earth shaking revelations, no lighting filled the sky, not even a clap of thunder. Not fully understanding that Gods promise to create a new heart in me that his Holy Spirit would then guide and instruct in my new life had just taken place.

It is at this point in my life I find this truth written in

> [John 17]
> ¹⁷Sanctify them through your truth your word is truth.

My spirit felt an urgent need to know more about GOD so I began a much deeper study of the Holy Scriptures. Being a babe in Christ I began to see how little I knew of God and how only the scriptures contain fully the revelations about him. Here I find my answer written in

> [Colossians2]
> ²That their hearts might be comforted, being knit together in love, and to all riches of the full assurance of understanding, to the acknowledgement of the mystery of God, and of the Father, and of Christ;
> ³And within them are hid all the treasures of wisdom and knowledge.

My studies were such a blessing I could hardly contain it. It was here my enemies became clear.

CHAPTER 4

The FLESH and SATAN

Of course my enemy's, the Flesh and Satan were present and were very busy revealing my fleshly lusts and casting many doubts about my new life. Having confessed Jesus as my savior before men, thoughts of what my friends would think about me or the do this and do not do that rushed through my mind. As I struggled on in the summer of 1960 God opened an impossible door and we purchased our first home in the city where I worked. My friend Kent invited and we joined a small group of believing Christians who held meetings in the local YMCA. The pastor was Jacob Watcher. Jacob was a godly teaching pastor. During the next few months the group grew in number and the decision was made to purchase land and build a church we would name Calvary Bible Church. As we members worked during our free time guided by a member [Glen Kilgore] who was a contractor, we built and moved into our new church within that year's time. I was baptized in the new baptismal. For a reason to be baptized first read of the great revival, as he prepared the way for Jesus, by John the Baptist written in

[Matthew 3]
⁵Then went out to him Jerusalem, and all Judaea, and the
entire region round about Jordan,
⁶Which were baptized of him in Jordan, confessing their sins.

The need to be baptized is made clear to me when I read what Paul called to be apostle to all gentiles did immediately after his conversion. Read here the story written in

[Acts 9]

¹⁷And Ananias went his way, and entered into the house; and putting his hands on him said, Brother Saul, the Lord, even Jesus, that appeared to you in the way that you came, has sent me, that you might receive your sight, and be filled with the Holy Ghost.

¹⁸Then immediately there fell from his eyes as it had been scales and he received sight forthwith, and arose, and was baptized.

The reason to be baptized is written in

[1 Peter 3]

²¹The like figure whereunto even baptism does also now save us (not the putting away of the filth of the flesh, but the answer of a good conscience toward God,) by the resurrection of Jesus Christ

²²Who is gone into heaven and is on the right hand of God; angels and authorities and powers being made subject to him.

And then this command of Jesus to his eleven disciples we find written in

[Matthew 28]

¹⁹Go you therefore, and teach all nations, baptizing them in the name of the Father, and of the Son, and of the Holy Ghost

²⁰Teaching them to observe all things whatsoever I have commanded you and, lo, I am with you always, even to the end of the world. Amen.

Within the churches there is still controversy over baptism. I find that scripture is oft times used out of its context. The apostle Paul did baptize, however because believers were saying I am of Paul; and I of Apollos; and I of Cephas; and I of Christ, I find the following Paul wrote can be taken out of context to say one need not be baptized written in

[1 Corinthians 1]

¹⁷For Christ sent me not to baptize but to preach the gospel not with wisdom of words to prevent the cross of Christ being made of none effect.

[18]Because the preaching of the cross is to them that perish foolishness; but to us which are saved it is the power of God.

Please understand at this point many will not say being born again one must be baptized, because baptism does not save you. It does however give one a good conscience toward God as written in

[1 Peter 3]
[21]The like figure whereunto even baptism does also now save us (not the putting away of the filth of the flesh, but the answer of a good conscience toward God,) by the resurrection of Jesus Christ

When born again I believe the Holy Ghost gives the heart this desire. That as soon as possible after being baptized by the spirit and born again from above, being baptized by water will show the world you believe your salvation has been confirmed by God. However I must point out this, written in

[Matthew 7]
[16]You shall know them by their fruits. Do men gather grapes from thorns, or figs from thistles?

My experience of knowing one that years ago claimed salvation and was baptized by water but is now clearly not saved, which along with this, tells me some claiming salvation will be baptized in water but will later show they have not been saved.

Months later I was asked to start teaching adult Sunday school classes. As membership grew, the next 7 years were filled with challenges and victories. During this time my faith grew stronger. After 7 years pastor Jacob announced Gods spirit had called him to serve another distant church. The new pastor we chose started out fine but soon discord arose within the church. Soon after this we left and joined a Baptist church. During the ensuing years we visited 4 other churches. This helped my progress in Christian growth. During this time the Holy Scriptures warning that the believer's life will have trials and tribulations proved very true. This period in my Christian growth resolved reemerging questions such as the following.

CHAPTER 5

Can The Saved Be Lost?

Jesus says none will be lost as written in

[St. John 10]

²⁷My sheep hear my voice, and I know them, and they follow me

²⁸And I give to them eternal life; and they shall never perish; neither shall any man pluck them out of my hand.

²⁹My Father, which gave them me, is greater than all; and no man is able to pluck them out of my Father's hand.

³⁰I and my Father are one.

Now please read what Jesus tells Nicodemus written in

[John 3]

³Jesus answered and said to him, truly, truly, I say to you, except a man be born again, he cannot see the kingdom of God.

⁴Nicodemus said to him, how can a man be born when he is old? Can he enter the second time into his mother's womb, and be born?

⁵Jesus answered, truly, truly, I say to you, except a man is born of water and of the Spirit, he cannot enter into the kingdom of God.

First let me say there are many professing salvation that may not be saved. By way of explanation, if I am a single man and put on a wedding ring proclaiming I am married does that make it true? No, because I cannot prove it. I use this to emphasize it is written in

[Matthew 7]
    ¹⁶You shall know them by their fruits.

Now and in other places the scriptures tell us that once one has been born of water by a woman they must be then born again by the spirit from above to be saved. And thereby become a son of God with Jesus Christ their Lord and Master they can know beyond doubt they have eternal life and are protected by Gods Angels.

CHAPTER 6

Gods Angels

The Holy Word of God from Genesis to Revelation tells the work Angels do serving God in his plan for man. In my studies, it is my opinion; there are 3 basic divisions of this innumerable host. One third serve God at his throne, one third serve Gods actions with man and one third serve Satan. This being said let us now explore what Angels are. It is written they are spirits

> [Psalms 104]
> ⁴Who makes his angels spirits; his ministers a flaming fire.

They are called the sons of God as written in

> [Job 1]
> ⁶Now there was a day when the sons of God came to present themselves before the Lord and Satan came also among them.

They are also called sons as written in

> [Job 38]
> ⁷When the morning stars sang together, and all the sons of God shouted for joy?

They are very powerful as written in

[2 Kings 19]

[33]By the way that he came, by the same shall he return, and shall not come into this city, said the Lord.

[34]For I will defend this city to save it for mine own sake and for my servant David's sake.

[35]And it came to pass that night, that the angel of the Lord went out, and smote in the camp of the Assyrians an hundred fourscore and five thousand and when they arose early in the morning, behold, they were all dead corpses.

They can destroy as written in

[1 Chronicles 21]

[15]And God sent an angel unto Jerusalem to destroy it and as he was destroying, the Lord beheld, and he repented him of the evil, and said to the angel that destroyed, It is enough, stay now your hand. And the angel of the Lord stood by the threshing floor of Ornan the Jebusite.

They are subject to Jesus as written in

[1 Peter 3]

[22]Who is gone into heaven and is on the right hand of God; angels and authorities and powers being made subject unto him.

They also worship Jesus written in

[Hebrews 1]

[6]And again when he brings in the first begotten into the world he says and let all the angels of God worship him.

In this present Age of Grace let us now explore how the angels serve Jesus in dealing with mankind's desire to know Jesus as savior. Be assured scripture tells us God is not willing that any perish however of all called to Jesus only a few will be saved. The reason so many fail to reach salvation in Jesus is primarily due to mans freewill that permits iniquity to come into his heart along with Satan and his angels working to stop Jesus from achieving total victory over Satan and mankind. Next, know that the churches have angels as written in

> [Revelation 1]
> [20]The mystery of the seven stars which you saw in my right hand and the seven golden candlesticks. The seven stars are the angels of the seven churches and the seven candlesticks which you saw are the seven churches.

The lord's angel protects believers written in

> [Psalms 34]
> [7]The angel of the Lord encamps round about them that fear him and delivers them.

They protect those born again as written in

> [Psalms 91]
> [11]Because he shall give his angels charge over you, to keep you in all your ways.
> [12]Angels shall bear you up in their hands, lest you dash your foot against a stone.
> [13]You shall tread upon the lion and adder the young lion and the dragon shall you trample under feet.
> [14]Because he has set his love upon me, therefore will I deliver him I will set him on high, because he has known my name,
> [15]He shall call upon me, and I will answer him I will be with him in trouble; I will deliver him, and honor him.
> [16]Also with long life I will satisfy him, and show him my salvation.

One might ask do we see angels today; yes it does happen even sometimes as written in

> [Hebrews 13]
> [1]Let brotherly love continue.
> [2]Do not forgetful to entertain strangers, for thereby some have entertained angels unawares.

Let no one persuade you the angels do not exist see

[Colossians 2]
[18]Let no man beguile you of your reward in a voluntary humility and worshipping of angels, intruding into those things which he hath not seen, vainly puffed up by his fleshly mind,

Perhaps this might surprise some to know this is written in

[1 Corinthians 6]
[3]Know you not that we shall judge angels? How much more things that pertain to this life?

Yes we worship good angels and shall judge evil angles. The fallen angels are described in

[Revelation 12]
[3]Then there appeared another wonder in heaven, and behold a great red dragon, having seven heads and ten horns and seven crowns upon his heads.
[4]And his tail drew the third part of the stars of heaven and did cast them to the earth and the dragon stood before the woman who was ready to be delivered, for to devour her child as soon as it was born.
[5]Then she brought forth a man child, who was to rule all nations with a rod of iron and her child was caught up to God and to his throne.

Described in other parts of scripture the dragon and stars are Satan and his angels. It was in the second dispensation of God before the flood the angels of Satan did this written in

[Genesis 6]
[1]So it came to pass, when men began to multiply on the face of the earth, and daughters were born unto them,
[2]That the sons of God saw the daughters of men that they were fair; and they took them wives of all which they chose.

³And the Lord spoke, my spirit shall not always strive with man, for that he also is flesh yet his days shall be an hundred and twenty years.

⁴There were giants in the earth in those days; and also after that, when the sons of God came in to the daughters of men, and they bear children to them, the same became mighty men which were of old, men of renown.

⁵And God saw that the wickedness of man was great in the earth, and that every imagination of the thoughts of his heart was only evil continually.

⁶Thus it repented the Lord that he had made man for the earth and it grieved him at his heart.

It is my opinion knowing man was just starting to multiply and that all angels are also called sons of God that these were angels from Satan. The angels that took wives of all they chose created a line of giants in the land. These angels were cast into the bottomless pit where they await final judgment. Satan's remaining evil angels are used by God as written in

[Psalms 78]
⁴⁹He cast upon them the fierceness of his anger, wrath, and indignation, and trouble, by sending evil angels among them.

Or read about Saul written in

[1 Samuel 16]
¹⁴But the Spirit of the Lord departed from Saul and an evil spirit from the Lord troubled him.

Yes these evil spirits are evil angels used by God for his purposes such as written in

[Judges 9]
²³Then God sent an evil spirit between Abimelech and the men of Shechem; and the men of Shechem dealt treacherously with Abimelech

What many do not realize is that God uses evil to bring good to his believers. It may shock many to know God says he creates evil. In the entire written word of God this statement is written only in

> [Isaiah 45]
> ⁷I form the light, and create darkness I make peace, and create evil I the Lord do all these things.

Because the scriptures contain a vast number of times God uses his good and evil angels [spirits] in dealing with mans eternal destiny. One can see in this Age of Grace that using the angels to protect his born again believers God also makes every effort to reach mans conscience and freewill with the conviction that only Jesus can save their soul giving them eternal life in the world to come. Because God is not willing that any are lost to eternal damnation he freely gave us his son Jesus who paid the price of dying for the remission of our sins. Cleansed with a good conscience toward God, we who are born from above, look forward to see Jesus face to face in eternity.

CHAPTER 7

My Lifelong Learning Process

When I was born again, with a new heart, the Holy Spirit engaged with my spirit and began a lifelong learning process. Being born again I studied the scriptures and experienced an increase in the knowledge of God, the Holy Spirit and Jesus Christ.

I believe a path to increasing the knowledge of God should begin with one word.

[The word is ASK]

First read this written in

[Matthew 7]
⁷Ask, and it shall be given you; seek, and you shall find; knock, and it shall be opened to you
⁸Every one that asks receives and he that seeks finds and to him that knocks it shall be opened.

Be careful here. Ask What? Seek What? And Knock Why? I fear many will ask amiss because they do not understand the context, ASK is given in. Sadly, this can result in judgment written in

[Matthew 7]

²²Many will say to me in that day, Lord, Lord, have we not prophesied in your name? And in your name have cast out devils? And in your name done many wonderful works?

²³And then will I profess to them I never knew you depart from me you that work iniquity.

A careful study of Matthew 7 gives context to why we should ASK. The question now is who to ask.

We find the answer written in

[Romans 8]

¹There is therefore now no condemnation to them which are in Christ Jesus, who walk not after the flesh but after the Spirit.

This begs the question of what does it mean to walk in the spirit of Christ Jesus? The answer is found in the book of prophesies by Isaiah foretelling God sending his son Christ Jesus the Messiah to earth written in

[Isaiah11]

¹And there shall come forth a rod out of the stem of Jesse and a Branch shall grow out of his roots

²And the spirit of the Lord shall rest upon him, the spirit of wisdom and understanding, the spirit of counsel and might, the spirit of knowledge and of the fear of the Lord;

³And shall make him of quick understanding in the fear of the Lord and he shall not judge after the sight of his eyes neither reproves after the hearing of his ears

One can now see that walking in the spirit of "Christ Jesus" includes sharing the attributes of his spirit. The spirit of wisdom and understanding, the spirit of counsel and might, the spirit of knowledge and of the fear of the Lord;

It is the spirit of "Christ Jesus" that guides us in what to ASK, what to SEEK, and when to KNOCK.

As my wisdom and knowledge increased my faith grew stronger. Be assured there were many trials and tribulations along the way and still continue to this day. All believers must stay alert that, their trials and tribulations can stifle their learning process. Only by prayerfully studying the scriptures can one know what is good and what is evil as written in

> [Romans12]
> [1]I beseech you therefore, brethren, by the mercies of God, that you present your bodies a living sacrifice, holy, acceptable to God, which is your reasonable service.
>
> [2]And be not conformed to this world but be transformed by the renewing of your mind, so you may prove all that is the good, and acceptable, and perfect will of God.
>
> [3]For I say, through the grace given to me, to every man that is among you, not to think of himself more highly than he ought to think; but to think soberly, according as God has dealt to every man the measure of faith.

It is also written in

> [1Thessalonians5]
> [21]Prove all things; hold fast that which is good.

CHAPTER 8

My Questions Answered

Here are a few answers God has given me. Be assured there are more God has given me but I am only listing what I believe are the most critical for living in this present evil world. Being born again I find this exhortation written in

[1st Thessalonians 5]

[14]Now we exhort you brethren warn them that are unruly comfort the feebleminded support the weak and be patient toward all men.

[15]See that none render evil for evil to any man; but ever follow that which is good, both among your selves, and to all men.

[16]Rejoice evermore.

[17]Pray without ceasing.

[18]In everything give thanks for this is the will of God in Christ Jesus concerning you.

[19]Quench not the Spirit.

[20]Despise not prophesying.

[21]Prove all things; hold fast that which is good.

[22]Abstain from all appearance of evil.

[23]And the very God of peace sanctify you wholly; and I pray God your whole spirit and soul and body be preserved blameless to the coming of our Lord Jesus Christ.

During my years of scripture study many questions came to mind. God is faithful and the Holy Ghost revealed answers for many but not all I searched for. Here I wish to address a few that were revealed to me and pray it will help give a better understanding of how important scripture study is within "Jesus Bride". Those born from above are the Bride of Jesus. They are given the duty to help others in coming to Jesus to be saved.

First let me say I am aware Satan knows the scriptures better than anyone. Satan does not stop at the churches door. He goes in and many times all the way to the pulpit. I have learned to take no one's explanation of scripture as true unless the scriptures confirm it. Confirmation takes more than using a scripture verse while not understanding the whole context it is given in. I will address this in the following answers, but first let us examine evil.

CHAPTER 9

The Face of Evil

To deny that evil exists is pure foolishness. The bible from Genesis thru Revelation tells of countless acts and conditions where evil has occurred. In my studies I find evil is used by God even though it appears contrary to his will. It is here I find 3 basic evils. First there are, beyond count, many evil acts that man commits. Then there is a natural evil of earthquakes, disease, plagues, volcanoes and weather related storms. Thirdly there are evil spirits, Satan's fallen angels that can take possession with control of the bodies of humans. With such a vast array of evils it is here that Gods natural law he ordained, "For any action there is an opposite and equal reaction", helps me understand how and why God uses evil to produce good. This greatly magnifies the Eternal Glory of God.

For those asking why does evil exist or why does it happen, the answers are found in Gods holy bible. At first thought one might say evil exists because of Satan, preachers tell us he is evil. But where did Satan come from. The answer is he came from heaven. No matter how deep you look the final answer is God created evil. The reason evil exists is written in

> [Romans 3]
> ⁵But if our unrighteousness commends the righteousness of God what shall we say? Is God unrighteous who takes vengeance? (I speak as a man)

Here we have mans unrighteousness showing Gods righteousness which shows us without evil how can man know who God is or understand his power and right to rule over his creation. Written only in Isaiah God tells us he created evil

> [Isaiah45]
> ⁶That they may know from the rising of the sun, and from the west, that there is none beside me. I am the Lord, and there is none else.
> ⁷I form the light, and create darkness I make peace, and create evil I the Lord do all these things.

And so by design I find God has created evil to use for his purposes. This helps me understand why this is such an evil world we live in as written in

> [Galatians 1]
> ³Grace be to you and peace from God the Father, and from our Lord Jesus Christ,
> ⁴Who gave himself for our sins, that he might deliver us from this present evil world, according to the will of God and our Father

Now having established that evil exists let us look to see what the scriptures say about the 3 basic evils.

CHAPTER 10

Evil "Immoral" Acts of Man

Yes an evil world with wicked people being created as written in

[Proverbs 16]
³Commit your works to the Lord, and your thoughts shall be established.
⁴The Lord has made all things for himself yes even the wicked for the day of evil.

For an example of created evil consider what is written that God said to Pharaoh. Or for good what Joseph said to his brothers in Egypt. Start with this written in

[Exodus 9]
¹⁵For now I will stretch out my hand that I may strike you and your people with pestilence; and you shall be cut off from the earth.
¹⁶Because in absolute deed for this cause have I raised you up, for to show in you my power; and that my name may be declared throughout all the earth.

Yes Pharaoh was created evil. Now read how God uses evil to produce good as told by Joseph, written in

[Genesis 50]
¹⁹And Joseph said to them, Fear not for am I in the place of God?

20Then as for you, you thought evil against me; but God meant it to good, to bring to pass, as it is this day, to save much people alive.

God knowing man's heart does use evil for good. See what is written in Jeremiah about the heart of man

[Jeremiah17]
9The heart is deceitful above all things and desperately wicked who can know it?
10I the Lord search the heart; I try the reins, even to give every man according to his ways, and according to the fruit of his doings.

The example of God using evil for good told by Joseph in Egypt gives evidence to how God works. Despite all the evils in this world, God has given believers this promise written in

[Romans 8]
28And we know that all things work together for good to them that love God to them who are the called according to his purpose.
29Because whom he did foreknow, he also did predestinate to be conformed to the image of his Son, that he might be the firstborn among many brethren.

Rarely, if at all, do we understand or see how good can result from mans immoral or evil actions, however history is filled with God producing good from such evil actions, To his eternal praise and glory.

CHAPTER 11

Natural Evil

Natural evils, acts of nature, are used by God for his purposes such as told to Noah, written in

> [Genesis 6]
> [17]And, behold, I, even I, do bring a flood of waters upon the earth, to destroy all flesh, wherein is the breath of life from under heaven; and everything that is in the earth shall die.
> [18]However with you will I establish my covenant; and you shall come into the ark, you and your sons and your wife and your sons wives with you.

Also read what the 2 witnesses are given power to do during the tribulation period written in

> [Revelation 11]
> [6]These have power to shut, heaven that it rain not in the days of their prophecy and have power over waters to turn them to blood, and to strike the earth with all plagues, as often as they will.

Also read what Jesus tells us written in

> [Matthew 24]
> [6]And you shall hear of wars and rumors of wars see that you be not troubled for all these things must come to pass but the end is not yet.

[7]For nation shall rise against nation and kingdom against
kingdom and there shall be famines and pestilences and
earthquakes in different places.

Here let me note that recent natural events taking place have been huge as
well as bewildering, such as, a tornado destroying half a city then next day a
new tornado destroying the other half in Joplin, Mo., or a huge earthquake
reeking enormous damage in Japan, unexpected volcanoes erupting or a
flock of birds falling dead from the sky. Seeking mans attention history is
full of God using these natural evil events.

CHAPTER 12

Evil Spirits

To deny possession by evil spirits is to reject God and his holy word as well as man's history.

Here read an example of God dealing with Saul as written in

> [1 Samuel 16]
> [14]But the Spirit of the Lord departed from Saul and an evil spirit from the Lord troubled him.

Now having possession the spirit is finally exorcised as written in

> [1 Samuel 16]
> [23]And it came to pass, when the evil spirit from God was upon Saul, that David took a harp, and played with his hand so Saul was refreshed, and was well, and the evil spirit departed from him.

Or consider the account of Paul written in

> [Acts 19]
> [11]And God wrought special miracles by the hands of Paul
> [12]So that from his body were brought to the sick handkerchiefs or aprons, and the diseases departed from them, and the evil spirits went out of them.

Now read what happens to novices that have not Gods permission also written in

[Acts 19]

[13]Then certain of the vagabond Jews, exorcists, took upon them to call over them which had evil spirits the name of the Lord Jesus, saying, we adjure you by Jesus whom Paul preaches.

[14]And there were seven sons of one Sceva a Jew and chief of the priests which did so.

[15]And the evil spirit answered and said Jesus I know and Paul I know; but who are you?

[16]And the man in whom the evil spirit was leaped on them, and overcame them and prevailed against them, so that they fled out of that house naked and wounded.

It seems clear to me these examples clearly show evil spirits should never be trifled with, rather only confronted by Gods chosen believers.

And though believers may not understand evil events taking place around them they can rest in the assurance it is part of Gods plan bringing good to them and glory to God.

Because I was inspired to write this after hearing a sermon by John Macarthur about [Why does evil dominate the world], concerning all the above and the vast amount of references I did not use I can only shout, To GOD BE THE GLORY.

CHAPTER 13

Mans Conscience

When God created heaven and its host he gave all freewill and an unconfirmed conscience. The Holy Word of God tells us Satan and a third of the angels using their freewill chose to not have a good conscience toward God, thus they fell from his grace while all others were confirmed having a good conscience toward God. Adam and Eve in the garden having freewill with an unconfirmed conscience toward God enjoyed fellowship with him in the garden. Exercising their freewill they failed Gods test to be confirmed by eating the forbidden fruit and thus fell from Gods grace. And so from Adam all mankind born are born in sin with freewill and a conscience that knows what is good and what is evil. It is here and in other parts of this book the conscience with scripture references are given. It is written all are born in sin in

[Psalms 51]
5Behold, I was shaped in iniquity; and in sin did my mother conceive me.

The Pharisees said this to Jesus written in

[John 9]
34They answered and said unto him, you were altogether born in sins, so how can you teach us? And they cast him out.

To understand the sinner's conscience convicts as does the believers, please read the story about Jesus and the woman that was taken in adultery written in

[John 8]

7So when they continued asking him, he lifted up himself, and said to them, He that is without sin among you, let him first cast a stone at her.

8Then again he stooped down, and wrote on the ground.

9And they which heard it, being convicted by their own conscience, went out one by one, beginning at the eldest, even to the last and Jesus was left alone, and the woman standing in the midst.

10When Jesus had lifted up himself, and saw none but the woman, he said to her, Woman, where are those that accused you? Has no man condemned you?

While these men were living under the Law of Moses also know the gentiles have this law written in their hearts, as written in

[Romans 2]

14For when the Gentiles, which have not the law, do by nature the things contained in the law, these having not the law, are a law to themselves

15Which show the work of the law written in their hearts, their conscience also bearing witness, and their thoughts the mean while accusing or else excusing one another;

Knowing you are born again and have complete freedom in Jesus, you must take special care not to weaken or defile your brethrens conscience as written in

[1 Corinthians 8]

9But take heed lest by any means this liberty of yours become a stumbling block to them that are weak.

10For if any man see one which has knowledge sit at meat in the idol's temple, shall not the conscience of him which is weak be emboldened to eat those things which are offered to idols;

11And through ones knowledge shall the weak brother perish that Christ died for?

12But when you sin so against the brethren and wound their weak conscience you sin against Christ.

What if the believer is invited to a meal and must go. The answer is written in

> [1 Corinthians 10]
> 27If any of them that believe not bid you to a feast, and you are disposed to go; whatsoever is set before you, eat, asking no question for conscience sake.
> 28But if any man says to you, this is offered in sacrifice to idols, eat not for his sake that showed it, and for conscience sake because the earth is the Lord's, and the fullness thereof
> 29Conscience, I say, not your own, but of the other for why is my liberty judged of another man's conscience?
> 30 For if I by grace am a partaker why am I evil spoken of for that for which I give thanks?

The reason for the accusing or else excusing one another is written in

> [Titus 1]
> 15To the pure all things are pure but to them that are defiled and unbelieving is nothing pure; but even their mind and conscience is defiled.
> 16They profess that they know God but, in works they deny him, being abominable, and disobedient, to every good work reprobate.

That which was true then I find so much more taking place today as written in

> [1 Timothy 4]
> 1Now the Spirit speaks expressly, that in the latter times some shall depart from the faith, giving heed to seducing spirits, and doctrines of devils;
> 2Speaking lies in hypocrisy; having their conscience seared with a hot iron;

While this continues accelerating believers should know God remains faithful and finds acceptable this, written in

[1 Peter 2]

[19]While this is thankworthy, if a man for conscience toward God endure grief, suffering wrongfully.

[20]Because, what glory is it, if, when you are buffeted for your faults, you shall take it patiently? But if, when you do well, and suffer for it, you take it patiently, this is acceptable with God.

Believers who suffer for well doing should know this is written in

[1 Peter 3]

[15]But sanctify the Lord God in your hearts and be ready always to give an answer to every man that asks you a reason of the hope that is in you with meekness and fear

[16]Having a good conscience; that, whereas they speak evil of you, as of evildoers, they may be ashamed that falsely accuse your good conversation in Christ.

[17]Because it is better, if the will of God be so, that you suffer for well doing, than for evil doing.

Having given the first reference to conscience found in John 8. v 9. Let us now read the last reference given in scripture, written in

[1 Peter 3]

[21]The like figure where even baptism does also now save us (not the putting away of the filth of the flesh, but the answer of a good conscience toward God,) by the resurrection of Jesus Christ

[22]Who is gone into heaven and is on the right hand of God; angels and authorities and powers being made subject to him.

Between the first and last reference to conscience found in Gods Holy Bible, John 8 and 1 Peter 3, one will find many references about mans conscience and the effect it has on mans freewill and actions he takes because of it. Knowing the earth and its fullness are the Lords with all children being born by the grace of God. It is the conscience that can guide one to eternal life with God and his son Jesus Christ in eternity. It is my opinion that many start life's journey exercising their freewill by doing things their conscience tells them is wrong. This can lead to their heart becoming hardened toward God and will lead to a growing weakening that eventually will become a defiled conscience. Thus as the years pass it becomes much more difficult if even impossible for them to see the light of truth in Gods Holy Word that only Jesus can save them from the fires of hell. While some say they are hell bent to go there, let them go. Such thoughts by believers are sin and a grave offence to God. For as it is written God is not willing that any should perish, he is still the God of miracles. Such thoughts show believers are not fulfilling Gods will in performing the duties God has given them to do.

And so I write the forgoing to those truly born again that knowing once saved you cannot be lost, however by not fulfilling Gods will their will be a loss of reward in eternity. Because salvation is open to all and considering today's world events it is apparent Gods church needs a sweeping revival else how many will be lost that might have been saved?

CHAPTER 14

What is Iniquity?

Start with this written in

> St. Mathew 24
> [12]And because iniquity shall abound, the love of many shall
> wax cold.

During the 1970's within a 7 year period I would occasionally search for the answer to the meaning of this word "Iniquity". Many said it was sin but if it is only sin why not say sin. My spirit said yes sin but a very special type of sin. I finally found my answer written in

> [1st Samuel 15]
> [23]And rebellion is as the sin of witchcraft and stubbornness
> is as iniquity and idolatry. Because you hast rejected the word of
> the Lord he has also rejected you from being king.

Sadly I realize Iniquity and Idolatry are a spiritual Stubbornness toward God. By putting Stubbornness and Idols first in life [That which controls one's life] helps explain the multitude of religions and churches found throughout the world. Man only wants Jesus Christ on mans terms not on Gods terms. Mans freewill and history show man does not want a sovereign God ruling over him. And so I fear many within the world's religions and churches on judgment day will expect to hear Jesus say welcome. It is however written Jesus tells the world what he will say in

[Matthew 7]

[19]Every tree that brings not forth good fruit is hewn down, and cast into the fire.

[20]Wherefore by their fruits you shall know them.

[21]Not every one that says to me, Lord, Lord, shall enter into the kingdom of heaven; but he that does the will of my Father which is in heaven.

[22]Many will say to me in that day, Lord, Lord, have we not prophesied in your name? And in your name have cast out devils? And in your name done many wonderful works?

[23]Then will I profess to them I never knew you depart from me, you that work iniquity.

It is also written in

[St. Luke 13]

[23]Then one said to Him, "Lord, are there few who are saved?" And He said to them,

[24]"Strive to enter through the narrow gate, for many, I say to you, will seek to enter and will not be able.

[25]"When once the Master of the house has risen up and shut the door, and you begin to stand outside and knock at the door, saying, 'Lord, Lord, open for us,' and He will answer and say to you, 'I do not know you, where you are from,'

[26]"Then you will begin to say, 'we ate and drank in your presence, and you taught in our streets.'

[27]"But He will say, 'I tell you I do not know you, where you are from. Depart from me, all you workers of iniquity.'

[28]"There will be weeping and gnashing of teeth, when you see Abraham and Isaac and Jacob and all the prophets in the kingdom of God, and yourselves thrust out.

And so these vivid descriptions by Jesus are of professing believers who walk not in the spirit of Christ Jesus. They still walk in the flesh claiming salvation while stubbornly giving their idols first place ahead of God.

CHAPTER 15

Do Believers Sin?

Yes, many times, even in ways we are not aware of. The believer must not look back to past sins because God has created a new heart in the believer cleansing it of all past sins, which will be remembered no more. Rather look to ones daily need for cleansing as we continue on the path to eternal life. Please note why Jesus washed the disciples' feet as written in

> [John 13]
> ¹⁰Jesus said to him, He that is washed only needs to wash his feet, but is clean every whit and you are clean, but not all.

Understand here Judas feet were washed and he then went out and betrayed Jesus. Because he did not return and confess his sin his soul was lost. Believers who sin and are convicted by the Holy Ghost should immediately repent and confess to God to maintain their fellowship with him. John speaking to believers writes in

> [1st John 1]
> ⁷But if we walk in the light as He is in the light we have fellowship with one another and the blood of Jesus Christ His Son cleanses us from all sin.
> ⁸If we say that we have no sin, we deceive ourselves, and the truth cannot be in us.
> ⁹If we confess our sins, He is faithful and just to forgive us our sins and to cleanse us from all unrighteousness.

[10]If we say that we have not sinned, we make Him a liar, and
His words are not in us.

Thus having our hearts cleansed we need daily cleansing of our [feet] contact with this sinful world as we walk salvations path because we are not of the world as written in

[John 15]
[19]If you were of the world, the world would love his own but because you are not of the world, but I have chosen you out of the world, therefore the world hates you.

When Jesus returns to claim his believers he will perform the final cleansing by giving them a new body clean and righteous to present to God his father.

CHAPTER 16

Same Sex Marriage

Over time man has learned that by changing the words he speaks he can make evil things appear acceptable to others or good things seem trivial. This has reached the point that today many times good is called evil and evil is called good. The result is mankind changes how he performs certain sinful acts in life. An example would be in times long past unwanted babies were killed by throwing them alive into the fires of Molech. Today man uses abortion. Mankind knows this makes it more acceptable to those who do not know God. Same sex marriage is a result of the base lust found in everyone. The history of this lust showed up in the story of Lot and God destroying Sodom & Gomorra. First it is written God says this in

> [Genesis 18]
> [20]And the Lord said, because the cry of Sodom and Gomorrah is great, and because their sin is very painful to them.
> [21]I will go down now, and see whether they have done altogether according to the cry of it, which is come to me; and if not, I will know.

Note the cry of Sodom in the Jewish Bible notes says this. Or, 'the cry of Sodom,' indicating the cry of its victims. (See Ramban, Ibn Ezra; Radak).

Also read what is written, before God heard this cry, from Sodom and Gomorrah written in

[Genesis 13]

¹³But the men of Sodom were wicked and sinners before the Lord exceedingly.

We now know why God destroyed Sodom and Gomorrah. The next story is written in

[Judges 19]

¹⁴Then they passed on and went their way; and the sun went down upon them when they were by Gibeah, which belongs to Benjamin.

The location being given as the tribe of Benjamin, we now read the old man's story written in

[Judges 19]

²⁰And the old man said, Peace be with you; howsoever let all your wants be left to me; only lodge not in the street.

²¹Then he brought him into his house and gave provender to the asses and they washed their feet, and did eat and drink.

²²Now as they were making their hearts merry, behold, the men of the city, certain sons of Belial, beset the house round about, and beat at the door, and spoke to the master of the house, the old man, saying, Bring forth the man that came into your house, that we may have sex with him.

²³And the man, the master of the house, went out to them, and said to them, No, my brethren, no, I pray you, do not so wickedly; seeing that this man is come into mine house, do not this folly.

²⁴Behold, here is my daughter a maiden, and my concubine; them I will bring out now, and humble you them, and do with them what seems good to you but to this man do not so vile a thing.

²⁵But the men would not listen to him so the man took his concubine, and brought her forth to them; and they raped her, and abused her all the night until the morning and when the day began to spring, they let her go.

²⁶Then came the woman in the dawning of the day, and fell down at the door of the man's house where her lord was, until it was light.

²⁷And her lord rose up in the morning, and opened the doors of the house, and went out to go his way and, behold, the woman his concubine was fallen down at the door of the house, and her hands were upon the threshold.

²⁸He then said to her, Up, and let us be going. But she did not answer. The man then placed her upon an ass, and the man mounted up, and rode him to his place.

²⁹And when he was come into his house, he took a knife, and laid hold on his concubine, and divided her, together with her bones, into twelve pieces, and sent her into all the coasts of Israel.

³⁰And it was so, that all that saw it said, There was no such deed done nor seen from the day that the children of Israel came up out of the land of Egypt to this day consider of it, take advice, and speak your minds.

Israel did speak as written in

[Judges 21]
⁶And the children of Israel repented them for Benjamin their brother, and said, There is one tribe cut off from Israel this day.

Saying the tribe of Benjamin was cut off was the result of a very bloody war between the 11 tribes and Benjamin's tribe. So bloody that all the cities and people of Benjamin were destroyed except for 600 men of Benjamin that survived. Israel then provided a way for the 600 men to capture wives from the gentiles to resume building up the tribe and cities of Benjamin.

It is here in m opinion the story foreshadows the Age of Grace when Judas betrayed Jesus Christ and Jesus then ordained Paul as apostle to the gentiles.

I find two results present from this story. One is the gentiles still retained their lust for deviate sexual acts which passed again to Israel because the 600 men of Benjamin captured and married gentile wives.

Now let us look to our present Age of Grace and see what God now says about sin and sinful deviate sexual acts. We find this written in

[Romans 1]

[17]For therein is the righteousness of God revealed from faith to faith as it is written, the just shall live by faith.

[18]Because the wrath of God is revealed from heaven against all ungodliness and unrighteousness of men, who know the truth but are unrighteous;

[19]Because that which may be known of God is manifest in them; for God has showed it to them.

[20]For the invisible things of him from the creation of the world are clearly seen, being understood by the things that are made, even his eternal power and Godhead; so that they are without excuse

[21]Because that, when they knew God, they glorified him not as God, neither were thankful; but became vain in their imaginations, and their foolish hearts were darkened.

[22]Professing themselves to be wise, they became fools,

[23]And changed the glory of the not corruptible God to an image made like to corruptible man, and to birds, and four-footed beasts, and creeping things.

[24]Wherefore God also gave them up to uncleanness through the lusts of their own hearts, to dishonor their own bodies between themselves

[25]Who changed the truth of God into a lie, and worshipped and served the creature more than the Creator, who is blessed forever. Amen.

[26]For this cause God gave them up to vile affections for even their women did change the natural use into that which is against nature

[27]And likewise also the men, leaving the natural use of the woman, burned in their lust one toward another; men with men working that which is unseemly, and receiving in themselves payment for their error which is deserved.

[28]And even as they did not like to retain God in their knowledge God gave them over to a reprobate mind, to do those things which are not convenient;

²⁹Being filled with all unrighteousness, fornication, wickedness, covetousness, maliciousness; full of envy, murder, debate, deceit, malignity; whisperers,

³⁰Backbiters, haters of God, despiteful, proud, boasters, inventors of evil things, disobedient to parents,

³¹Having no understanding, covenant breakers, without natural affection, implacable, unmerciful

³²Who knowing the judgment of God, that they which commit such things are worthy of death, not only do it, but they have pleasure in those that do them.

Thus by changing the words to make it acceptable, a lie is still a lie and same sex marriage is a lie. For therein is still committed the deviate sexual acts that God hates.

Can one escape this judgment of death? Yes, for this age of grace, first do this as written in

[John 3]
³Jesus answered and said to him, truly, truly, I say to you, except a man be born again, he cannot see the kingdom of God.

Then do this as written in

[Romans 13]
¹²The night is far spent, the day is at hand. let us therefore cast off the works of darkness, and let us put on the armor of light.

¹³Let us walk honestly, as in the day; not in rioting and drunkenness, not in chambering and wantonness, not in strife and envying.

¹⁴But put you on the Lord Jesus Christ and make not provision for the flesh to fulfill the lusts thereof.

One can also read how God feels about such things in Leviticus 20 wherein God gave Moses the statutes for Israel that those who commit such deviate sexual acts during the Mosaic Law period were to be put to death. Today I find they have so changed the words to make it so acceptable that in the name of, Freedom of Religion, many have even been ordained to preach from the pulpit.

To those who commit such acts today know this. If those of deviate sexual persuasion choose this path to certain destruction of their soul, so be it, However because we are still in, The Age of Grace, if any repent and turn to Jesus Christ to be, born from Above, they can escape the eternal damnation that awaits their current soul's condition.

CHAPTER 17

Is Abortion Murder?

Many have struggled with this question, does a fetus have life? Yes it does. It is written in

> [Leviticus 17]
> 14For it is the life of all flesh; the blood of it is for the life thereof therefore I said to the children of Israel, You shall eat the blood of no manner of flesh for the life of all flesh is the blood thereof whosoever eats it shall be cut off.

Because a fetus has blood it also has life. Here please know in the statutes under the covenant God made with Noah that is perpetual to all generations, found in Genesis 9. 12, that to shed mans blood resulted in a death sentence. Also in the 10 commandments God says, [Thou shall not kill]. This law of God is still in effect today. For those who do not agree take note because we have been given a freewill God also requires each person to be personally responsible for their actions. Does this mean if one has had an abortion they cannot be saved? No, all one need do is turn to the Lord Jesus Christ in repentance confessing all sin and ask Jesus to save you.

That none be cast out is written in

> [1st St. John 6]
> 37All that the Father gives me shall come to me; and whosoever that comes to me I will in no wise cast out.

That God is not willing any should perish is written in

> [2 Peter3]
> ⁹The Lord is not slack concerning his promise as some men count slackness but is longsuffering to us-ward, not willing that any should perish but that all should come to repentance.

Salvations door is open to all, however only those forsaking everything but God and his son Jesus can be born from above and can come in and be saved.

CHAPTER 18

Gentiles are called Dogs

If one is not a Jew then one can only be a Gentile. Understanding Gentile history explains why God calls them dogs. Gentile decadence and idolatry described before the flood, which also continues to this day is written in

> [Genesis 6]
> 5Then the Lord saw that the wickedness of man was great on the earth and that all the intent of the thoughts of his heart was only evil continually.
> 6Then the Lord was sorry that He had made man, on the earth, so He was grieved in His heart.

And so we find Gentiles are called Dogs throughout the scriptures.

To know gentiles are called dogs read this written in

> [Isaiah 56]
> 8It is the Lord God, who gathers the outcasts of Israel, says, "Yet I will gather to him others besides those who are gathered to him."
> 9All you beasts of the field, come to devour, all you beasts in the forest.
> 10His watchmen are blind, they are all ignorant; they are all dumb dogs that cannot bark; sleeping, lying down, and loving to slumber.

¹¹Yes, they are greedy dogs, which never have enough. And they are shepherds who cannot understand; they all look to their own way, every one for their own gain, from their own territory.

¹²"Come," one says, "I will bring wine, and we will fill ourselves with intoxicating drink; tomorrow will be as today, and much more abundant."

Please understand the promise to gather others, makes a promise to the Gentile race that God would open the door of faith to them. In his travels Jesus fulfilled Gods promise to the Gentiles and opened salvations door as written in

[Matthew 15]

²²They beheld, a woman of Canaan came from that region and cried out to Him, saying, "Have mercy on me, O Lord, Son of David! My daughter is severely demon-possessed."

²³But He answered her not a word. And His disciples came and urged Him, saying, "Send her away, for she cries out after us."

²⁴But He answered and said, "I was not sent except to the lost sheep of the house of Israel."

²⁵Then she came and worshiped Him, saying, "Lord, help me!"

²⁶But He answered and said, "It is not good to take the children's bread and throw it to the little dogs."

²⁷And she said, "True, Lord, yet even the little dogs eat the crumbs which fall from their masters' table."

²⁸Then Jesus answered and said to her, "O woman, great is your faith! Let it be to you as you desire." And her daughter was healed from that very hour.

And so the promise in [Isaiah 56.8] is being fulfilled as written in

[Romans11]

²⁵For I do not desire, brethren, that you should be ignorant of this mystery, lest you should be wise in your own opinion, that hardening in part has happened to Israel until the fullness of the Gentiles has come in.

CHAPTER 19

Evolution

The evolution theory has taken hold in today's world. I believe it to be the work of Satan because it denies Gods creation story in Genesis. Evolution scientists say the dinosaur became extinct 60 to 70 million years ago. If you ask how the scientists can determine the dinosaur bones are 60 to 70 million years old you will be told it is determined by the age of the sediment it is found in. If you ask how the sediment's age is determined you will be told by the age of the bones. This seems to be a perfect circle, like a dog chasing It's tail. Evolution scientists will not accept that God created fruit trees with fruit on day 3 of creation then created light on day 4. God says he did, do you believe God or Satan?

This creation account is written in

[Genesis1]
   ¹¹Then God said, "Let the earth bring forth grass, the herb that yields seed, and the fruit tree that yields fruit according to its kind, whose seed is in itself, on the earth"; and it was so.
   ¹²And the earth brought forth grass, the herb that yields seed according to its kind, and the tree that yields fruit, whose seed is in it according to its kind. And God saw that it was good.
   ¹³So the evening and the morning were the third day.
   ¹⁴Then God said, "Let there be lights in the firmament of the heavens to divide the day from the night; and let them be for signs and seasons and for days and years;

¹⁵"And let them be for lights in the firmament of the heavens to give light on the earth"; and it was so.

¹⁶Then God made two great lights the greater light to rule the day, and the lesser light to rule the night. He made the stars also.

¹⁷God set them in the firmament of the heavens to give light on the earth,

¹⁸And to rule over the day and over the night and to divide the light from the darkness. And God saw that it was good.

¹⁹So the evening and the morning were the fourth day.

Nor will evolution scientists explain how the largest dinosaur that ever lived was only a scant 3500 years ago and not the 60 to 70 million years they claim. It was estimated to weigh 200,000 pounds. So big it had to lie in a swamp. It ate vegetation that floated down to it at the mouth of the Jordan River where it enters the Dead Sea.

Here is Jobs description written in

[JOB40]

¹⁵Behold now behemoth, which I made with thee; he eats grass as an ox.

¹⁶Lo now, his strength is in his loins, and his force is in the navel of his belly.

¹⁷He moves his tail like a cedar the sinews of his stones are wrapped together.

¹⁸His bones are as strong pieces of brass; his bones are like bars of iron.

¹⁹He is the chief of the ways of God he that made him can make his sword to approach unto him.

²⁰Surely the mountains bring him forth food, where all the beasts of the field play.

²¹He lies under the shady trees in the covert of the reeds and fens.

²²The shady trees cover him with their shadow; the willows of the brook compass him about.

²³Behold, he drinks up a river, and hurries not he trusts that he can draw up Jordan into his mouth.

²⁴He takes it with his eyes his nose pierces through snares.

Read more about this giant leviathan in Job 41. Also know this giant leviathan was still seen approximately 1000 years later as written in

> [Psalms 104]
> ²⁵So is this great and wide sea wherein are things creeping innumerable, both small and great beasts.
> ²⁶There go the ships there is that leviathan, which you have made to play therein.

Also, can the evolution scientists explain how a river in south Texas flooded and exposed bedrock where the footprints of 2 dinosaurs and Mans footprint was revealed? I do not believe it was 70 million years old. Even the evolution scientist's estimate mans habitation to only be between 10,000 and 37000 years. I think their estimate of mans age is also incorrect.

Finally the evolution scientist's say we are evolving, however, God says everything is dying. The following is written in

> [Isaiah 51]
> ⁶Lift up your eyes to the heavens, and look upon the earth beneath for the heavens shall vanish away like smoke, and the earth shall wax old like a garment, and they that dwell therein shall die in like manner but my salvation shall be forever, and my righteousness shall not be abolished.

And finally evolution theory scientists cannot explain from the big bang theory how the universe has been discovered to be one long wave in the shape of Gods outstretched hand, or where the moon came from and how it originated, or how Gods law of gravity works. Or where the air breathing whale came from or what caused the multiple layers of sediment to develop, that are impossible to create by hydraulic action, which we find in the Grand Canyon or why skeletons of sea creatures are found in the mountains.

It is outrageous that this scientifically UN provable theory of evolution has become so acceptable to mankind that it is now taught in our schools.

CHAPTER 20

Context

To take a scripture out of context is sin. Doing so demeans God and the Lord Jesus. Reading the scriptures leading up to a particular scripture verse provides an understanding of it and its use. I have heard it said when 2 agree on anything if they ask God he will do it. If 2 ask God to save a loved one will he do it? No, God does not usurp mans free will. If 2 ask God to open that person's heart to the truth will he do it? Although it may take years of praying with much longsuffering, God will endeavor to answer YES as written in

[2 Peter3]
⁹The Lord is not slack concerning his promise as some men
count slackness but is longsuffering to us-ward not willing that
any should perish but that all should come to repentance.

The key is to pray within the will of God. If you read the story where 2 asking is written you will find it is telling about a brother sinning against you as written in

[St. Mathew 18]
¹⁵Moreover if your brother sins against you, go and tell him
his fault between you and him alone. If he hears you, you have
gained your brother.
¹⁶"But if he will not hear you, take with you one or two
more, that 'by the mouth of two or three witnesses every word
may be established.'

[17]"And if he refuses to hear them, tell it to the church. But if he refuses even to hear the church, let him be to you like a heathen and a tax collector.

[18]"Assuredly, I say to you, whatever you bind on earth will be bound in heaven, and whatever you loose on earth will be loosed in heaven.

[19]"Again I say to you that if two of you agree on earth concerning anything that they ask, it will be done for them by My Father in heaven.

[20]"For where two or three are gathered together in my name, I am there in the midst of them."

We must take special care using a scripture that it is not taken out of context. To do so is a sin. Please refer to the segment [ASK] for a better understanding of what [2 agree on anything] means. Always remember, we are not the message, we are just the messengers.

CHAPTER 21

Gethsemane

We read this story written in

[Mathew 26]

[36]Then came Jesus with them to a place called Gethsemane, and said to the disciples, Sit you here, while I go and pray yonder.

[37]Then he took with him Peter and the two sons of Zebedee, and began to be sorrowful and very heavy.

[38]Then said he to them, My soul is exceeding sorrowful, even until death tarry ye here, and watch with me.

[39]And he went a little further, and fell on his face, and prayed, saying, O my Father, if it be possible, let this cup pass from me nevertheless not as I will, but as thou wilt.

[40]Then he came to the disciples, and finds them asleep, and says to Peter, What, could you not watch with me one hour?

[41] Watch and pray that you enter not into temptation the spirit indeed is willing, but the flesh is weak.

[42]He went away again the second time, and prayed, saying, O my Father, if this cup may not pass away from me, except I drink it, your will be done.

[43]And he came and found them asleep again for their eyes were heavy.

[44]Then he left them, and went away again, and prayed the third time, saying the same words.

[45]Then came he to his disciples, and said to them, Sleep on now, and take your rest behold, the hour is at hand, and the Son of man is betrayed into the hands of sinners.

It is here in my opinion Jesus faced his greatest temptation. Being both Gods son and man in the flesh I think it no wonder his soul is exceeding sorrowful, even unto death. Surely the flesh of man wants to live. Yes Jesus knew what his sacrifice would do for the world, the salvation of many, and the final destruction of Satan. This hour of temptation is a valuable lesson for all believers. Here Jesus shows us how great a struggle with the flesh we all may face. It is here Jesus shows us the answer as he prays saying, [O my Father, if it be possible, let this cup pass from me nevertheless not as I will, but as thou wilt] We must always pray within Gods perfect will because as Jesus says, [Watch and pray, that ye enter not into temptation the spirit indeed is willing, but the flesh is weak] And so we find we can escape from all temptations because of this promise written in

[1st Corinthians 10]
[13]There has no temptation taken you but such as is common to man but God is faithful, who will not suffer you to be tempted above what you are able; but will with the temptation also make a way to escape, that you may be able to bear it.

Because Jesus sacrificed himself on the cross believers now have this written in

[Hebrews 4]
[14]Seeing then we have a great high priest that is passed into the heavens, Jesus the Son of God; let us hold fast our profession.
[15]For we have not an high priest which cannot be touched with the feeling of our infirmities; but was in all points tempted like as we are, yet without sin.
[16]Let us therefore come boldly to the throne of grace that we may obtain mercy, and find grace to help in time of need.

CHAPTER 22

Today's Preachers and Teachers

Within this current Age of Grace I see the following.

Because iniquity abounds and the love of many has grown cold in this present evil world I write this to encourage all true believing preachers, teachers and all who are born again to keep the faith and stay true to Gods holy word. I can see it is still true today of this world that which was written long ago in

[2 Peter 2]
¹Because there were false prophets also among the people, even as there shall be false teachers among you, who privately shall bring in damnable heresies, even denying the Lord that bought them, and bring upon themselves swift destruction.
²And many shall follow their pernicious ways; because of them the way of truth shall be evil spoken of.
³Using covetousness they shall with feigned words make merchandise of you whose judgment now of a long time lingers not and their damnation slumbers not.

Also read why they falsely preach, written in

[Titus 1]
¹⁰Because there are many unruly and vain talkers and deceivers, especially those of the circumcision

[11]Whose mouths must be stopped, who subvert whole houses, teaching things which they ought not, for filthy lucre's sake.

Satan also takes part in preaching righteousness with his angles as written in

[2 Corinthians 11]
[14]And no marvel; for Satan himself is transformed into an angel of light.
[15]Therefore it is no great thing if his ministers also be transformed as the ministers of righteousness; whose end shall be according to their works.

The television has brought a great amount of false preachers and teachers, even some known to be involved in gay or lesbian relationships. Who also preach and teach from church pulpits, to make for filthy lucre's sake they gain riches while leading astray their followers. The reason they are successful is written in

[2 Timothy 4]
[3]Now the time will come when they will not endure sound doctrine but after their own lusts shall they heap to themselves teachers, having itching ears;
[4]And they shall turn away their ears from the truth, and shall be turned to fables.
[5]Be diligent and watch in all things, endure afflictions, do the work of an evangelist, make full proof of thy ministry.

Here let me say one must search the scriptures to confirm that the preaching or teaching being said is true. Because so many say, you can feel good by just believing Jesus and God will fix your problems or send you wealth and give whatever you ask for. However God promises to only provide your needs not your desires and Jesus says the believer's life will have trials and tribulations.

This being said let us now look to see what is written concerning preachers and teachers of Gods holy word starting with this command by Jesus to the 11 disciples written in

[Matthew 28]

[18]Then Jesus came and spoke to them, saying, all power is given to me in heaven and in earth.

[19]Go you therefore, and teach all nations, baptizing them in the name of the Father, and of the Son, and of the Holy Ghost

[20]Teaching them to observe all things whatsoever I have commanded you and, lo, I am with you always, even unto the end of the world. Amen.

Following this we find Jesus did this which is written in

[Ephesians 4]
[10]He that descended is the same also that ascended up far above all heavens, that he might fill all things.)

[11]And he gave some, apostles; and some, prophets; and some, evangelists; and some, pastors and teachers;

[12]Thereby perfecting the saints, for the work of the ministry, for the edifying of the body of Christ

[13]Till we all come in the unity of the faith, and of the knowledge of the Son of God, to a perfect man, to the measure of the stature of the fullness of Christ

This charge to preach the word of God is written in

[2 Timothy 4]
[1]I charge you therefore before God, and the Lord Jesus Christ, who shall judge the quick and the dead at his appearing and his kingdom;

[2]Preach the word; be instant in season, out of season; reprove, rebuke, exhort with all longsuffering and doctrine

[3]For the time will come when they will not endure sound doctrine; but after their own lusts shall they heap to themselves teachers, having itching ears;

For one not to preach the holy word is to be accursed as written in

[Galatians 1]
[8]Although we, or an angel from heaven, preach any other gospel to you than that which we have preached to you, let him be accursed.

What women should preach or teach has been in controversy from the beginning of this Age of Grace. This, about women, is written in

[1 Corinthians 14]

[33]Because God is not the author of confusion, but of peace, as in all churches of the saints.

[34]Let your women keep silence in the churches for it is not permitted to them to speak; but they are commanded to be under obedience, as also says the law.

[35]Therefore if they will learn anything let them ask their husbands at home for it is a shame for women to speak in the church.

Also written in

[1 Timothy 2]

[11]Let the woman learn in silence with all subjection.

[12]I suffer not a woman to teach nor to usurp authority over the man, but to be in silence.

[13]For Adam was first formed, then Eve.

I find that which women should teach is written in

[Titus 2]

[3]The aged women likewise, that they be in behavior as becomes holiness, not false accusers, not given to much wine, teachers of good things;

[4]That they may teach the young women to be sober, to love their husbands, to love their children,

[5]Being discreet, chaste, keepers at home, good, obedient to their own husbands, that the word of God be not blasphemed.

I am well aware of the firestorm this writing can create, however when has Gods word not resulted in unbelievers scorning his Holy Word. Please be assured I am not the message, but only the messenger. Concerning Preaching and teaching I am aware Satan knows the scriptures better than anyone. Satan does not stop at the churches door. Using his evil spirits he goes in and many times all the way to the pulpit. I have learned to take no one's explanation of scripture as true unless the scriptures confirm it. Confirmation takes more than using a scripture verse while not understanding the whole context it is given in. I have experienced hearing preachers and teachers both on T.V. and in churches smoothly make false statements about God and his Holy Word. The only answer I find to this dilemma is for believers to diligently search the scriptures that one might know the truth while gaining a fuller knowledge of God and his plan for man. Most critical to all the above, is only by careful study of the word of God can a believer grow in the grace and knowledge of God and his redeeming son Jesus Christ. Note I write redeeming son because Jesus is the ONLY SON that can save lost sinners also because all those born again are given the power to grow in grace and become the sons of God as written in

[John 1]
¹²But as many as received him, to them he gave the power to become the sons of God, even to them that believe on his name

Yes he gives the born again the power, however history shows many of God's chosen, having free will, behave like little children playing in his play house having little time or paying scant attention to Gods instructions. This conduct will be judged and result in loss of some of one's reward on judgment day as written in

[Revelation 22]
¹²So behold I come quickly; and my reward is with me, to give every man according as his work shall be.

Many preaching and teaching today fail in helping believers understand God commands them while living in this present evil world they must not be part of it as written in

[Romans 12]
¹I beseech you therefore, brethren, by the mercies of God, that you present your bodies a living sacrifice, holy, acceptable to God, which is your reasonable service.
²Then be not conformed to this world but be transformed by the renewing of your mind, so that you may prove what is that good, and acceptable, and perfect, will of God.

Keeping the mind renewed on God fends off Satan's attack because Gods word is not hidden as written in

[2 Corinthians 4]
3But if our gospel be hid, it is hid to them that are lost
4In whom the god of this world has blinded the minds of them which believe not lest the light of the glorious gospel of Christ who is the image of God should shine to them.

While the scriptures have a great deal to say about living in this evil world it also clearly tells why those saved should not be part of it. How this can be done is written in

[Ephesians 6]
11Put on the whole armor of God so that you may be able to stand against the wiles of the devil.
12For we wrestle not against flesh and blood but against principalities against powers against the rulers of the darkness of this world against spiritual wickedness in high places.

Knowing the ongoing evils committed in this world the believer should read this written in

[1 Timothy 6]
6But godliness with contentment is great gain.
7For we brought nothing into this world and it is certain we can carry nothing out.
8And having food and raiment let us be therewith content.

In view of all I have seen and heard in today's world it is my opinion Gods believing churches need to prayerfully seek God to send revival beginning with those now born again. For if a true revival comes it must start with God's people because those coming in to learn of Jesus need all the help and guidance the born again can give them. Within this age of grace history tells us they do fall away as written in

[Ephesians 4]
21If so be that you have heard him, and have been taught by him, as the truth is in Jesus

[22]That you put off concerning the former conversation the old man, which is corrupt according to the deceitful lusts;

[23]And be renewed in the spirit of your mind;

[24]And that you put on the new man who after God is created in righteousness and true holiness.

Once having learned about Jesus If one falls away it is impossible to renew them as written in

[Hebrews 6]

[4]For it is impossible for those who were once enlightened, and have tasted of the heavenly gift and were made partakers of the Holy Ghost!

[5]Who having tasted the good word of God, and the powers of the world to come,

[6]If they shall fall away, to renew them again to repentance; seeing they crucify to themselves the Son of God afresh and put him to an open shame.

It is terrible to see so many of God's chosen are disillusioned with life and Christianity, also because America is getting rid of Christianity from all public sites and erasing God from the schools of children and now talking about removing, In God We Trust, from our paper money, I believe God is currently judging the nation and unless America repents he will bring harsher judgment with increasing intensity to our nation. This shinning beacon to the world must turn back to God or be destroyed.

CHAPTER 23

The Lost Book of Esaias

The prophet Esaias is quoted many times in the New Testament, scholars say the book is really the book of Isaiah, however you will not find the book of Esaias or Esaias making his quotes anywhere in the Old Testament. This begs two questions, who is this prophet and where is his book to be found?

I have found a link to unravel this mystery so let us start with several New Testament quotes to develop context for the search starting with this writing in

[Matthew 3]
³For this is he that was spoken of by the prophet Esaias, saying, The voice of one crying in the wilderness, Prepare you the way of the Lord, make his paths straight.

Here we see the book did exist as written in

[Luke 4]
¹⁷And there was delivered to him the book of the prophet Esaias. And when he had opened the book, he found the place where it was written,
¹⁸The Spirit of the Lord is upon me, because he has anointed me to preach the gospel to the poor; he has sent me to heal the

brokenhearted, to preach deliverance to the captives, and recovering of sight to the blind, to set at liberty them that are bruised, [19]To preach the acceptable year of the Lord.

Now read what Jesus says Esaias prophesied to Israel as written in

[Mark 7]
[6]He answered and said to them, Well has Esaias prophesied of you hypocrites, as it is written, This people honored me with their lips, but their heart is far from me.
[7]Howbeit in vain do they worship me, teaching for doctrines the commandments of men.

Here is a vague clue to why the book of Esaias was lost. We find it written in

[Romans 9]
[27]Esaias also cried concerning Israel, Though the number of the children of Israel be as the sand of the sea, a remnant shall be saved
[28]For he will finish the work and cut it short in righteousness because a short work shall the Lord make upon the earth.
[29]And as Esaias said before except the Lord of Sabbath had left us a seed we had been as Sodom and been made like Gomorrah.
[30]What shall we say then? That the Gentiles, which followed not after righteousness, have attained to righteousness, even the righteousness which is of faith.
[31]But Israel which followed after the law of righteousness hath not attained to the law of righteousness.

It is here the clue to this mystery is written in

[Romans 11]
[25]For I would not, brethren that you should be ignorant of this mystery lest you should be wise in your own conceits; that blindness in part is happened to Israel until the fullness of the Gentiles be come in.

Having researched what this prophet says in the New Testament I then searched the Old Testament finding only bits and pieces of his quotes written by others which leads me to conclude the book was purposely lost by some action of God. I wonder if the book of Esaias contains the help Israel needs to recover from their blindness in part and be saved. In view of current events taking place in this evil world I believe this world is fast approaching the end of the Age of Grace. Be it known during the time I was finishing this writing the Fox News in a very short statement announced this [The book of Esaias has been found in the Dead Sea scrolls].

To all the above I can only say to all, Be Ready.

CHAPTER 24

The END TIMES

In view of recent world events it appears the world is fast approaching the end of [The Age of Grace] as written in

[2 Peter3]

[2]That ye may be mindful of the words which were spoken before by the holy prophets, and of the commandment of us the apostles of the Lord and Saviour

[3]knowing this first, that in the last days mockers shall come with mockery, walking after their own lusts,

[4]And saying where is the promise of his coming? for, from the day that the fathers fell asleep, all things continue as they were from the beginning of the creation.

[5]For this they willingly are ignorant of that by the word of God the heavens were of old and the earth standing out of the water and in the water

Next read this written in

[2 Timothy 3]

[1]This know also, that in the last days perilous times shall come.

²Because men shall be lovers of their own selves, covetous, boasters, proud, blasphemers, disobedient to parents, unthankful, unholy.

³Having no natural affection, trucebreakers, false accusers, incontinent, fierce, despisers of those that is good.

⁴Traitors, heady, high-minded, lovers of pleasures more than lovers of God;

⁵Having a form of godliness, but denying the power thereof from such turn away.

⁶For of this sort are they which creep into houses and lead captive silly women laden with sins led away with diver's lusts.

⁷Ever learning and never able to come to the knowledge of the truth.

The prophecies in the book of Daniel tell of spiritual battles we cannot see and earthly events and battles already fulfilled with future events to yet be fulfilled. While studying Daniel's prophecies and the book of Revelation I see many things matching these prophecies. Although from the beginning of Gods church each generation has felt it would see the end of the Age of Grace the following information leads me to conclude the world is now fast approaching the end of this Age of Grace. It is here I outline events leading me to make such a conclusion.

We begin with the ten kings of the fourth beast written in

[Daniel 2]

⁴¹And whereas you saw the feet and toes part of potter's clay and part of iron the kingdom shall be divided but there shall be in it of the strength of the iron forasmuch as you saw the iron mixed with miry clay.

⁴²And as the toes of the feet were part of iron, and part of clay, so the kingdom shall be partly strong, and partly broken.

⁴³And whereas you saw iron mixed with miry clay they shall mingle themselves with the seed of men but they shall not cleave one to another even as iron is not mixed with clay.

⁴⁴And in the days of these kings shall the God of heaven set up a kingdom which shall never be destroyed and the kingdom shall not be left to other people but it shall break in pieces and consume all these kingdoms and it shall stand for ever.

The next event is written in

[Daniel 7]

[7]After this I saw in the night visions, and behold a fourth beast, dreadful and terrible, and strong exceedingly; and it had great iron teeth it devoured and broke in pieces, and stamped the residue with the feet of it and it was di from all the beasts that were before it; and it had ten horns.

[8]I considered the horns, and, behold, there came up among them another little horn, by it there were three of the first horns plucked up by the roots and, behold, in this horn were eyes like the eyes of man, and a mouth speaking great things.

[9]I beheld till the thrones were cast down, and the ancient of days did sit, whose garment was white as snow, and the hair of his head like the pure wool his throne was like the fiery flame and his wheels as burning fire.

[10]A fiery stream issued and came forth from before him thousand thousands ministered unto him, and ten thousand times ten thousand stood before him the judgment was set, and the books were opened.

[11]I beheld then because of the voice of the great words which the horn spoke I beheld even till the beast was slain, and his body destroyed, and given to the burning flame.

This fourth beast with toes of iron and clay aptly describes Syria, Egypt, Lebanon, Saudi Arabia, Jordan, Yemen, Oman, Kuwait, Iraq and Omar of today. These kingdoms fear the little horn that speaks great things and are loosely united as described by the ten toes of iron and clay [Radical and Moderate Muslims]. Recent events taking place in the Middle East match the little horns description written in

[Daniel 11]

[21]And in his estate shall stand up a vile person to whom they shall not give the honor of the kingdom but he shall come in peaceably and obtain the kingdom by flatteries.

[22]And with the arms of a flood shall they be overrun from before him and shall be broken; yes also the prince of the covenant.

²³And after the league made with him he shall work deceitfully for he shall come up and shall become strong with a small people.

²⁴He shall enter peaceably even upon the fattest places of the province; and he shall do that which his fathers have not done, nor his fathers' fathers; he shall scatter among them the prey, and spoil, and riches yes, and he shall forecast his devices against the strong holds, even for a time.

²⁵And he shall stir up his power and his courage against the king of the south with a great army; and the king of the south shall be stirred up to battle with a very great and mighty army; but he shall not stand for they shall forecast devices against him.

²⁶Yes, they that feed of the portion of his meat shall destroy him, and his army shall overrun and many shall fall down slain.

²⁷And both these kings' hearts shall be to do mischief and they shall speak lies at one table but it shall not prosper for yet the end shall be at the time appointed.

²⁸Then shall he return into his land with great riches; and his heart shall be against the holy covenant; and he shall do exploits, and return to his own land.

²⁹At the time appointed he shall return and come toward the south; but it shall not be as the former or as the latter.

³⁰Because the ships of Chitin shall come against him therefore he shall be grieved and return and have indignation against the holy covenant so shall he do; he shall even return and have intelligence with them that forsake the holy covenant.

³¹And arms shall stand on his part and they shall pollute the sanctuary of strength and shall take away the daily sacrifice and they shall place the abomination that makes desolate.

³²And such as do wickedly against the covenant shall he corrupt by flatteries but the people that do know their God shall be strong and do exploits.

³³And they that understand among the people shall instruct many yet they shall fall by the sword and by flame by captivity and by spoil many days.

³⁴Now when they shall fall, they shall be helped with a little help but many shall cleave to them with flatteries.

[35]And some of them of understanding shall fall to try them and to purge and to make them white even to the time of the end because it is yet for a time appointed.

[36]And the king shall do according to his will; and he shall exalt himself, and magnify himself above every god, and shall speak marvelous things against the God of gods, and shall prosper till the indignation be accomplished for that that is determined shall be done.

[37]Neither shall he regard the God of his fathers, nor the desire of women, nor regard any god for he shall magnify himself above all.

[38]But in his estate shall he honor the God of forces and a god whom his father's knew not shall he honor with gold and silver and with precious stones and pleasant things.

[39]Thus shall he do in the most strong holds with a strange god, whom he shall acknowledge and increase with glory and he shall cause them to rule over many, and shall divide the land for gain.

[40]And at the time of the end shall the king of the south push at him and the king of the north shall come against him like a whirlwind, with chariots, and with horsemen, and with many ships; and he shall enter into the countries, and shall overflow and pass over.

[41]He shall enter also into the glorious land and many countries shall be overthrown but these shall escape out of his hand, even Edom and Moab and the chief of the children of Ammon.

[42]He shall stretch forth his hand also upon the countries and the land of Egypt shall not escape.

[43]But he shall have power over the treasures of gold and of silver and over all the precious things of Egypt and the Libyans and the Ethiopians shall be at his steps.

[44]But tidings out of the east and out of the north shall trouble him therefore he shall go forth with great fury to destroy and utterly to make away many.

[45]And he shall plant the tabernacles of his palace between the seas in the glorious holy mountain yet he shall come to his end and none shall help him.

This little horn, in my opinion, is Iranian president Mahmoud Ahmadinejad because he is doing the following.

1. Speaks great things, [Daniel 7-8].
2. Wants Israel destroyed, [Daniel 11-30].
3. Supplies the Palestinians with arms and money to battle Israel, [Daniel 11-24].
4. Paid to rebuild the Hezbollah homes destroyed in Lebanon's war with Israel, [Daniel 11-24].
5. Waged a four year war with Iraq with millions killed resulting in a stalemate with no winner, [Daniel 11-25]. With Saddam Hussein in control of Iraq it became necessary to remove him. The U.S.A. with Britain and others did remove Saddam resulting in a new Iraq government of the Persian religion, the same as Iran. With both Iraq and Iran now being Persians the stage is set for the little horn [Mahmoud Ahmadinejad] to uproot the three kingdoms, Iraq, Syria and Lebanon which opens the way to conquering Jerusalem as written in[Daniel 11-30 thru 39].
6. Going forth the little horn [Mahmoud Ahmadinejad] will conquer many countries including Egypt, but only so far as to be at the Libyans and the Ethiopians steps. It is here in my opinion knowing he is developing the missiles and atomic bomb that he will fulfill prophecy.

First read the location as written in

> [Revelation 17]
> ⁹And here is the mind which hath wisdom. The seven heads
> are seven mountains, on which the woman sits.

Scholars say this speaks of Rome which will be destroyed in one hour, also written in

> [Revelation 18]
> ⁹And the kings of the earth, who have committed fornication
> and lived deliciously with her, shall bewail her, and lament for
> her, when they shall see the smoke of her burning,
> ¹⁰Standing afar off for the fear of her torment, saying, Alas,
> alas, that great city Babylon [Rome], that mighty city! For in one
> hour is her judgment come.

I note here that America having started building a missile defense in Europe has stopped construction thus leaving Rome defenseless to his missile attack that results in a war which ends with his destruction shortly after the start of the 3 ½ years of trouble. I estimate his end within 220 days by subtracting the 2300 days from the 1 week period of trouble written in

[Daniel 8]
[14]And he said to me two thousand and three hundred days; then shall the sanctuary be cleansed.

[Daniel11-40 thru 45] tells of his end.

7. Also during this time of 3 ½ years of trouble God sends his two witnesses written in

[Revelation 11]
[2]And the court which is without the temple leave without, and measure it not; for it has been given to the nations and the holy city shall they tread under foot forty and two months.
[3]Because I will give to my two witnesses and they shall prophesy a thousand two hundred and threescore days, clothed in sackcloth.
[4]These are the two olive trees and the two candlesticks, standing before the Lord of the earth.
[5]And if any man desires to hurt them, fire proceeds out of their mouth and devours their enemies; and if any man shall desire to hurt them, in this manner must he be killed.
[6]These have the power to shut the heaven so that it rains not during the days of their prophecy and they have power over the waters to turn them into blood, and to strike the earth with every plague, as often as they shall desire.

After this the 3 &1/2 years of Great Tribulation begins, ending with the great battle known as Armageddon written in

[Revelation16]
[16]And he gathered them together into a place called in the Hebrew tongue Armageddon.

In my opinion Daniel 12 indicates the rapture will take place at the midpoint of this period of 7 years, just before the time of trouble such as never was written in

> [Daniel 12]
> [1]And at that time shall Michael stand up, the great prince which stands for the children of your people and there shall be a time of trouble, such as never was since there was a nation even to that same time and at that time your people shall be delivered, every one that shall be found written in the book.
> [2]And many of them that sleep in the dust of the earth shall awake, some to everlasting life, and some to shame and everlasting contempt.
> [3]And they that are wise shall shine as the brightness of the firmament; and they that turn many to righteousness as the stars forever and ever.

Currently many run to and fro and due to computers with the internet's networking I find knowledge has increased at a staggering rate. Thus I see the time of the end written in

> [Daniel 12]
> [4]But you O Daniel shut up the words and seal the book even to the time of the end many shall run to and fro and knowledge shall be increased.

Man has now come full circle as written in

> [Ecclesiastes 1]
> [9]The thing that has been it is that which shall be and that which is done is that which shall be done and there is no new thing under the sun.
> [10]Is there anything whereof it may be said, See, this is new? It has been already of old time, which was before us.
> [11]There is no remembrance of former things; neither shall there be any remembrance of things that are to come with those that shall come after.

I know many of the events given in Daniels Prophecy took place before Jesus was born, however, because of Ecclesiastes 1. 9, and present world events I believe it shall happen again, because history repeats itself. However, this time in fullness to the end of this Age of Grace. It is for this reason and because of the vast knowledge available to man as written in Daniel 12. The foregoing reasons lead me to believe we are at The End Times door because of the computer which does convert and resolves the language barrier easily. So that man can now do anything he imagines to do, just as it was at the Tower of Babel written in

[Genesis11]
⁵And the Lord came down to see the city and the tower which the children of men built.

⁶And the Lord said Behold the people are one and they have all one language; and this they begin to do and now nothing will be restrained from them which they have imagined to do.

At this point one can see that Satan, who controls this world's kingdom, has worked thru the ages establishing his version of mans knowledge. Thus, without restraint, man can now do anything he imagines to do. With mans willful disobedience to Gods sovereign rule and Satan knowing all that God has foretold in the Holy Scriptures the unsaved souls and Satan are working steadfastly to prevent the Lord Jesus Christ from returning to reclaim Gods kingdom on earth. The effort of Satan and man to stop Jesus from returning will fail, because we read Isaiah saw the lord's return written in

[Isaiah 2]
¹The word that Isaiah the son of Amoz saw concerning Judah and Jerusalem.

²And it shall come to pass in the last days, that the mountain of the Lord's house shall be established in the top of the mountains, and shall be exalted above the hills; and all nations shall flow unto it.

³And many people shall go and say, Come all, and let us go up to the mountain of the Lord, to the house of the God of Jacob; and he will teach us of his ways, and we will walk in his paths for out of Zion shall go forth the law, and the word of the Lord from Jerusalem.

[4]And he shall judge among the nations and shall rebuke many people and they shall beat their swords into plowshares and their spears into pruning hooks nation shall not lift up sword against nation; neither shall they learn war any more.

We find the promise of his coming written in Revelation scripture verses 7 and 20

[Revelation 22]
[7]Behold, I come quickly blessed is he that keeps the sayings of the prophecy of this book.
[20]He that testifies these things says, surely I come quickly. Amen. Even so, come, Lord Jesus.

CHAPTER 25

Will America Survive?

In this world America has for years now been on the same path that the world is on, which leads to vast corruption in high places. This path has lead to removing God from first place [ONE NATION UNDER GOD]. Be assured God always judges sin and America is now being judged. Consider the condition of America as seen in Billy Graham's Prayer for America.

THIS MAN SURE HAS A GOOD VIEW OF WHAT'S HAPPENING TO OUR COUNTRY!

'Heavenly Father, we come before you today to ask your forgiveness and to seek your direction and guidance. We know Your Word says, 'Woe to those who call evil good,' but that is exactly what we have done. We have lost our spiritual equilibrium and fed our values. We have exploited the poor and called it the lottery. We have rewarded laziness and called it welfare. We have killed our unborn and called it choice. We have shot abortionists and called it justifiable . . . We have neglected to discipline our children and called it building self esteem. We have abused power and called it politics. We have coveted our neighbor's possessions and called it ambition. We have polluted the air with profanity and pornography and called it freedom of expression. We have ridiculed the time-honored values of our forefathers and called it enlightenment. Search us, Oh God, and know our hearts today; cleanse us from sin and Set us free. Amen!'

With time fast approaching the end, America still has 2 choices.

America can continue its current path and be DESTROYED or REPENT AND BE SAVED.

CHAPTER 26

My Future

Abraham looked for a "city built by God" I also seek that city written in

[Hebrews 1]
8By faith Abraham obeyed when he was called to go out to the place which he would afterward receive as an inheritance. And he went out, not knowing where he was going.

9By faith he sojourned in the land of promise as in a foreign country dwelling in tents with Isaac and Jacob, the heirs with him of the same promise;

10For he waited for the city which has foundations whose builder and maker is God.

And as the world continues to reject my Lord and Master Jesus Christ I continue on as written in

[1st Peter 2]
1Therefore, laying aside all malice, all guile, hypocrisy, envy, and all evil speaking,

2Being newborn babies desire the pure milk of the word that you may grow thereby.

3If indeed you have tasted that the Lord is gracious.

4Coming to Him as to a living stone, rejected indeed by men, but chosen by God and precious,

⁵You also, as living stones, are being built up a spiritual house, a holy priesthood, to offer up spiritual sacrifices acceptable to God through Jesus Christ.

⁶Therefore it is also contained in the Scripture, "Behold, I lay in Zion a chief cornerstone, elect, precious, and he who believes on Him will by no means be put to shame."

⁷To you therefore which believe he is precious but to them which be disobedient, the stone which the builders disallowed, the same is made the head of the corner.

⁸And a stone of stumbling and a rock of offence even to them which stumble at the word being disobedient whereunto also they were appointed.

⁹But you are a chosen generation, a royal priesthood, an holy nation, a peculiar people; that you should show forth the praises of him who has called you out of darkness into his marvelous light;

Be aware God has given a, conscience, to each person born into this world and he will judge all sinners as written in

[Romans2]

¹³(For not the hearers of the law are just before God, but the doers of the law shall be justified.

¹⁴Because when the Gentiles which have not the law do by nature the things contained in the law these having not the law find it is a law within themselves

¹⁵Which show the work of the law written in their hearts their conscience also bearing witness and their thoughts the mean while accusing or else excusing one another ;

During my life's journey to this point I have seen many changes. Yes wars, disasters and conflicts but much more such as technological developments. Man going to the moon was huge but in its time so were things such as the Farm Tractor replacing the horse or the Clock Radio replacing the Alarm Clock or the Automatic Washer replacing the hand powered Ringer or the Refrigerator replacing the Ice Box or Television or the battery operated Calculator or the Computer which, as foretold in the book of Daniel, has brought a vast increase in mans knowledge. With God having poured out such a vast treasure of blessings upon this world the only change I have not seen within this lifetime of improvements and changes is the vast multitude of men having free will and a conscience to know what is good and what is evil still refuse to accept Jesus as their savior or God as this worlds Sovran ruler. As for myself, I shall continue in faith and trust serving my Lord and Master Jesus Christ while living in this sinful world but not part of it. Ever looking forward to that Glorious point I shall see him Face to Face.